Genre Nonfiction

Essential Question
Why do we celebrate holidays?

MW00723669

by Francine Thompson

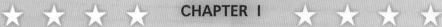

CHAPTER I

What Is Labor Day?

In the United States, Labor Day is a special day. It happens in September.

On Labor Day, many grown-ups do not go to work. Children do not go to school.

Labor Day is on the first Monday of September.

calendar

SEPTEMBER

Sunday	Monday	Tuesday	Wednesday	Thursday	Friday	Saturday
				1	2	3
4	5	6	7	8	9	10
11	12	13	14	15	16	17
18	19	20	21	22	23	24
25	26	27	28	29	30	

factory

Long ago, children worked in places like this.

Did you ever wonder what Labor Day is? Labor Day is a day to honor workers.

In the past, the work day was very long. Workers could not rest. Young children had to work, too. Sometimes work was not safe.

3

Now our nation has laws. The laws make sure that workers are safe. Work is more fair. A worker can <u>take a break</u>.

Other laws say that children can't work. Children must go to school.

In Other Words   rest. En español: *descansar.*

Hard hats keep workers safe.

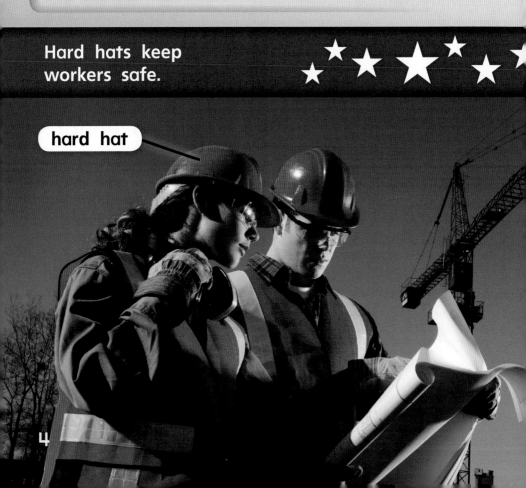

hard hat

4

cafeteria worker

Many workers help us at school.

Americans unite to say thank you to workers on Labor Day.

People also like to celebrate on Labor Day!

STOP AND CHECK

Why do we celebrate Labor Day?

CHAPTER 2

How Do We Celebrate?

Some cities <u>have</u> parades on Labor Day. It's fun to wave a flag. Maybe some clowns will surprise you. Have you ever gone to a parade?

Language Detective	<u>Have</u> is a special verb. Find another special verb on page 4.

Parades are fun!

flag

parade

blanket

Some concerts are held outdoors.

In some towns, people can listen to music after a Labor Day parade. The town has a concert. The whole family has fun.

Strike up the band!

In Other Words Get the band started!
En español: *empezar a tocar.*

On Labor Day, families like to have picnics. They share their food at a park. What is your favorite picnic food?

It's fun to eat lunch outside.

grill

8

Relaxing with family can also be fun.

After lunch, people like to relax for a few minutes. Then it's time to play a game! What games do you like to play outside?

A lot of people go to the beach on Labor Day. It's fun to play in the sand. When it gets hot, it's time to go in the ocean. Don't forget <u>your</u> swimsuit!

Language Detective	<u>Your</u> is a possessive pronoun. Find another possessive pronoun on page 8.

Many families like the beach. ★★★★★

ocean

sand

Many children ride the bus to school.

Labor Day is at the end of summer. The next day, most children go to school. It's time to use a backpack again.

Here comes the bus!

STOP AND CHECK

What are some fun things to do on Labor Day?

Respond to Reading

Retell

Use your own words to retell *It's Labor Day!*

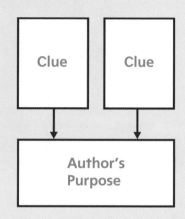

Text Evidence

1. Why did the author include the photo on page 3? Author's Purpose

2. Why did the author write this book? Author's Purpose

3. How do you know that *It's Labor Day!* is nonfiction? Genre

Compare Texts
Read about another American
holiday.

Four Voyages

ship

Christopher Columbus

Columbus Day is on the second Monday in October.

Christopher Columbus sailed from Spain. Columbus made four voyages, or trips, to the Americas. On Columbus Day, we remember the first voyage.

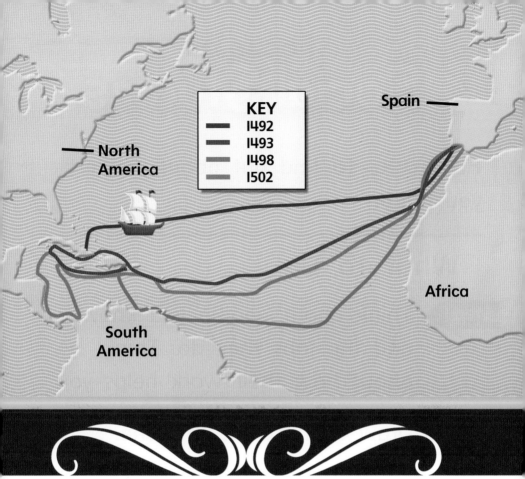

KEY
1492
1493
1498
1502

Spain

North America

Africa

South America

The map shows all four voyages. You can see where the ships went.

Make Connections
Look at both selections. How do you celebrate both holidays? Text to Text

Focus on
Social Studies

Purpose To find out about workers you honor

What to Do

Step 1 ▶ Think about people you know and the jobs they do. Think about how their work helps you.

Step 2 ▶ Draw a chart like this one. Fill it in with the jobs those people do.

Jobs	I honor them because
teachers	They help me learn.

Step 3 ▶ Write a paragraph about someone in your chart. Draw a picture. Share with the class.